21-Day Journal

A Journey of Personal Transformation

459 N. Gilbert Rd. Suite C-210
Gilbert, AZ 85234
www.BestLifeMedia.com
480-926-2287

Second paperback edition: January 2016
Library of Congress Control Number: 2015934608
ISBN: 978-1-935127-32-1

Train your body so that
change feels better than habit.

– ILCHI LEE

Your
21-Day
Journey

Congratulations on your choice to make positive changes in your life! Whatever kind of change you want to make during the next 21 days, I'm certain you will experience the incredible sense of hope, energy, and joy that comes from reunion with yourself.

I am excited because I know all the great things that are going to happen for you. I know they will happen because they happened to me during the many 21-day trainings I have experienced, including the one at Moak Mountain in Korea.

In many Asian traditions, 21 days is considered a spiritually significant time period. Ancient sacred texts often describe the transformation of spiritual figures through 21 days of ascetic discipline. Some experts tell us that it takes at least 21 days to create a new habit because of the time required for new neural connections to form in the brain.

You may face many challenges and obstacles during your 21-day training. But never give up!

Obstacles are great opportunities for you to have greater understanding and awareness of yourself. Make any obstacle your chance to improve.

Always choose positive things. Keep giving good information and messages to yourself. Good information makes a good brain. You are the master of your brain. Your brain belongs to you, not to someone else or a particular environment. Always keep this in mind, and tell your brain what you really want to do and what you really want to be.

Journaling helps you clarify your thoughts and feelings, and it helps you formulate a new understanding of yourself. Use this journal not only as a diary of your training, but as a record of the life lessons you don't want to forget. We remember what we record.

No matter what kind of 21-day training you are in now, you will eventually ask yourself who you are, what you are doing, and why.

Explore how you feel about your life, and write about how you are changing and growing or not growing.

In practicing any 21-day training, you will realize that you are on a spiritual journey. All of us are on this journey. If you realize this, any 21-day training will lead you toward a lifelong journey of completion.

– ILCHI LEE

Your Brain & Your Habits

Did you know that any mind-body training is really about your brain?

Your brain is the creator of everything in your life. All the neural connections in your brain come together in a unique way to create the unique person that you are. These connections are responsible for your personality, your talents, your emotions, everything that makes you you.

Undoubtedly, there are many great things about your brain that are an asset to your life. It is the source of your talents and all the emotions that make your life rich and abundant. But there may be a few things about your brain that you're not crazy about–things that disrupt your life or leave you feeling dissatisfied with your life. Any 21-day training with Body & Brain Yoga or Brain Education principles is essentially about taking actions that help you rewire your brain in a way that will make your life more satisfactory to you.

If you are considering any 21-day training, then you probably have some habit in mind that you want to change. Chances are, it is something you have already tried to work on in the past. You may wonder why it has been so hard to change this part of yourself, even though you want it so badly.

The reason is simply that your brain is not yet wired in the way it needs to be to accommodate the behavior you want. That is why it takes real commitment to accomplish the changes you want to make. If your brain is already wired to accommodate a set of less-than-ideal behaviors, it is almost as if your brain is working against you when you want to change a behavior.

The good news is that we can effectively rewire our brains. The human brain has an ability known as neuroplasticity, which means that the brain is able to change its neural connections. It is this feature of the brain that gives you power over your habits and the ability to change them.

Developing a good habit will require determination, focus, and time. Although the time it takes to change a habit may depend on many factors, experts agree that neural connections can be well established with three weeks of diligent repetition.

Show yourself that you are capable of keeping a promise to yourself for 21 days.

This is the very least that you owe to yourself when you do any 21-day training.

Any 21-day training, physical strength, emotional well-being, spiritual awakening . . . whatever focus it has, will help you take control of your brain and control of your life. Use your 21-day training to create a brain that supports the life of your dreams.

Your Self-declaration

I'd like to introduce a tool that you can use throughout your 21-day training. It is a self-declaration–the voice of creation. A declaration is not an explanation or description. It is not tied to comparison or circumstance. It is pure choice. Your declaration reflects your being, here and now. No reasons or justifications are necessary.

Self-declaration is one of the most powerful ways to express your passionate goal or purpose. Your declaration creates a new possibility. Listening to your inner voice as thoughts and emotions recede into the background, you journey to the place of infinite possibility, the place of a new beginning. From there, you declare yourself to the universe.

Create your self-declaration to help keep your brain infused with the will to complete your 21-day training. How do you create your self-declaration?

All you need to do is create a simple declarative sentence that will keep your mind in a positive state.

In other words, it is a statement that helps you be the kind of person who naturally embodies the goal you are seeking. This statement is not the same as the goal itself: it is a statement of character, a simple "I am" statement.

This statement may be in direct opposition to the negative self-talk that is too often produced by your brain. For example, if your brain has habitually undermined your dieting attempts with thoughts like "I am ugly" or "I have bad genes," then please replace this with a strong statement in the reverse, such as "I am beautiful" or "I am so healthy." If you have a non-I am statement such as "I can do it" or " I love myself," that is absolutely okay, just go with it. Surprisingly, you will discover your self-declaration if you listen to your inner voice. If it comes to you, just accept and grasp it. Again, no reasons or justifications are necessary.

It may be tempting to create more than one, but please choose just one that resonates most deeply with you. Once you have discovered your declaration, write it down in your journal. Say it over and over. Talk to a supportive friend or a mentor about the life you envision. Declare yourself consistently, diligently, and sincerely. Your declaration is truth.

My Self-Declaration

. . . .

. . . .

. . . .

. . . .

. . . .

. . . .

. . . .

. . . .

. . . .

. . . .

. . . .

the Skill of Watching

It is often said that the journey matters more than the destination. The process of your 21-day training is no different. The most important thing you can get from your training is not the achievement of the goal itself, but the greater understanding and awareness of yourself that comes through the process of achieving it.

Watching yourself with absolute honesty is the best way to gain understanding about yourself. Watching means developing your ability to see underneath the surface of your own actions and emotions to discover your underlying needs and motivations. This may sound simple enough on the surface, but it is really a skill that must be perfected through constant practice.

Watching yourself honestly can be difficult because there is often a profound difference between who we think we are on the outside and who we truly are on the inside. Most of us have some image of who we think we are, but this may be highly affected by external influences, such as social status and cultural preconceptions. Identity labels such as "professional," "mom," or "athlete" help us make our way in the world and live the lives we want to live. The problem is that most of us behave as though these are the things that actually give us the ultimate value. It is almost as if we truly believe that these labels are who we are.

In terms of your self-development, you might say, "I want to improve my relationships" or "I want to lose weight." But an important question you should ask yourself is, "Why do I want this thing?" If the answer is strictly external, such as "I'm sick of arguing" or "I want to look better," you will have a hard time developing the will needed to make changes. To gain genuine will, you need to go deeper than that.

Get down below the outer layers of yourself to your inner core through the skill of watching. Pay attention to dimensions of yourself that are seldom observed or known–that is, your own deepest, inner levels.

Anything you do, do it with full attention. Watch your thoughts and feelings with calm awareness and clear intention.

When we are able to see things as they are, without the filter of thoughts or preconceived ideas, it is called "detached watching." By doing this, you will be able to anchor your will to something far more solid than surface desires, and you will find greater inspiration toward your growth.

As you go through your day, watch what is going on inside yourself. You may notice certain emotions and thoughts attached to various actions that you take. Note any inner dialogue and notice what events trigger certain thoughts that may undermine your growth. Some thoughts or feelings are pleasant, some unpleasant or painful, often dwelling on the past or looking hopefully, or anxiously, to the future. When these things happen, it is easy to push them away or suppress them. However, avoid making any judgments about the rightness or wrongness of these things—just watch them. At the end of each day, make a list of your awakenings about yourself in your journal.

Contract
with Myself

I, the undersigned, commit the next 21 days to achieving the following goals without reservation and with complete sincerity.

....

....

....

....

....

....

Your Name   ....

Date   ....

There is a difference between doing something
with sincerity and just doing it without sincerity.
With sincerity, we become immersed in the here and now;
our minds don't run off to the past and the future.
Sincerity allows us to achieve what we desire.

Day 1

A New Beginning

Awareness of the present moment
makes every moment a new beginning,
a new opportunity.

Day 1

Tomorrow's Plan

....
....
....
....
....
....
....
....
....
....
....
....
....
....
....
....
....

No matter who we were up to just a moment ago,
no matter what situation we were in, nothing
can detract from our new choice in this moment.
Nothing in the past can diminish the sacredness
of the present.

Day 2

Signals from the Body

When you are sensitive and responsive
to the signs and rhythms of your body,
you are more deeply connected to the rich,
wonderful texture of all life experience.

Day 2

Tomorrow's Plan

....

....

....

....

....

....

....

....

....

....

....

....

....

....

....

....

Signals from the body–a butterfly in the stomach,
a tingling in the toes, or even pain or discomfort–
can take on meanings related to creative urges
or spiritual growth.

Day 3

You Deserve It

Don't believe anyone who tells you
that you are not good enough
or do not deserve the life you want.

Day 3

Tomorrow's Plan

....

....

....

....

....

....

....

....

....

....

....

....

....

....

....

The most important thing you create is
your own life. It is critical that you empower
yourself to create the life you want.
Don't ignore your own creative genius and
do not turn over the creation of your life to others.

Day 4

Garden of Your Mind

Your mind possesses
the highest level of sensors
and can pick up on every thought.

Day 4

Tomorrow's Plan

....

....

....

....

....

....

....

....

....

....

....

....

....

....

....

....

Whatever seeds of thought you sow
in the garden of your mind,
whether negative or positive,
they inevitably grow and blossom.

Day 5

A Specialist

There is no expert for human experience.
Each of us is the specialist of our lives.

Day 5

Tomorrow's Plan

....
....
....
....
....
....
....
....
....
....
....
....
....
....
....

We have no idea when and how our lives
first began. What is more important is that
we are each given our own life.
You have the right and responsibility
to choose how you will use it.

Day 6

Profound Respect

What did you see in the mirror this morning?
Your face? Your age? A success or a failure?
These are not everything you are. Occasionally
close your eyes and try to see what is invisible.

Day 6

Tomorrow's Plan

. . . .

. . . .

. . . .

. . . .

. . . .

. . . .

. . . .

. . . .

. . . .

. . . .

. . . .

. . . .

. . . .

. . . .

. . . .

Give yourself profound respect—a feeling that
you are extremely valuable. Those who
experience this can make positive choices
in the face of countless alternatives.

Day 7

Your Senses and Sensibilities

Taking care of yourself,
being in charge of your life,
is a way of saying you are worthwhile,
an acknowledgment of your self-worth.

Day 7

Tomorrow's Plan

. . . .

. . . .

. . . .

. . . .

. . . .

. . . .

. . . .

. . . .

. . . .

. . . .

. . . .

. . . .

. . . .

. . . .

. . . .

. . . .

. . . .

You must awaken to the many inherent sensibilities and
sensitivities of your body and be able to feel when you
are moving toward health or away from it.

Day 8

Choices and Responsibility

We are each, as individuals, uniquely responsible
for the lives we live. There is no one else who should
take responsibility for your choices.

Day 8

Tomorrow's Plan

....

....

....

....

....

....

....

....

....

....

....

....

....

....

....

....

You may not be able to create or control all
of the events that affect your life,
but you can create and control your responses
to everything that you experience.

Day 9

Only Now

If you think about a mulberry tree while standing in front of a pine tree, you cannot smell the fresh scent that the pine tree is generously sharing with you.

Day 9

Tomorrow's Plan

....

....

....

....

....

....

....

....

....

....

....

....

....

....

....

....

....

Do not slide into the past or flow into the future.
The Now is all you have. Allow this present moment to
grow and grow until it shines bright light on
the past and the future, and only the Now remains.

Day 10

Your Character

True emptiness is full of energy waving minutely.
You should be careful not to run because of too much
anxiousness, but be even more careful not to be lazy.
Silence and insensibility are different.

Day 10

Tomorrow's Plan

....
....
....
....
....
....
....
....
....
....
....
....
....
....
....

A once-in-a-blue-moon choice does not speak to your character. A countless number of choices will create a habit, out of which the flower of your character will bloom. Good character is a fruit borne of a tree of good habits.

Day 11

Your Journey, Your Story

You can compare your life to a journey,
but more often than not it is closer
to a wandering. When you have a clear idea
of who you are and why you live,
then your life becomes a journey.

Day 11

Tomorrow's Plan

··
··
··
··
··
··
··
··
··
··
··
··
··
··
··
··
··

When you have a passionate life purpose,
a story is created about your life. And when the end
comes, even if the story adds up to only one line,
the story reaches a settled conclusion.

Day 12

Everything Is Transient

Change is the only changeless reality. Seasons,
livelihoods, personal relationships
—all of these will change. By meditating
on this truth, you recognize that you, too,
are a manifestation of transience.

Day 12

Tomorrow's Plan

· ·

When you understand transience deeply,
you become humble and sincere. You treasure
each moment and endeavor to do your best.
You feel less stress and become more accepting
of the diverse phenomena of life.

Day 13

You Are in Charge

Life need not occur as an experience
that is happening to you. It can be
an experience that is happening through you.
You can place yourself in charge.

Day 13

Tomorrow's Plan

....

....

....

....

....

....

....

....

....

....

....

....

....

The true meaning of responsibility lies in
accepting that you are the creator. It means
understanding and accepting that you create your
circumstances and your experience. Responsibility does
not mean passive acceptance or resignation,
but dignity and authority.

Day 14

It's All Right

True creativity comes from clear understanding of your passionate life purpose. When things don't go as you wish, you need to review the purpose with your mind emptied, instead of only focusing on methods of resolution.

Day 14

Tomorrow's Plan

You have something inside that is steady, even among your many emotions that come and go with your life's joys and sorrows. At the center of your consciousness, a being quietly watches you. When you are struggling in despair, that being gives you strength not to give up and stirs your hope by saying, "It's all right."

Day 15

Blossom Fully

Do not wear your weaknesses as a burden.
Let your imperfections become the foothold
on which you can climb.

Day 15

Tomorrow's Plan

....

....

....

....

....

....

....

....

....

....

....

....

....

....

....

A flower that is afraid of withering will never blossom
into the beauty that is its potential.
Flowers are born for the purpose of blossoming.
Always be a fully blossomed flower
living in the moment.

Day 16

No Action, No Creation

One day of planning is better than ten of praying.
One day of action is worth more than ten of planning.
Creation takes place only when knowledge
is moved into action.

Day 16

Tomorrow's Plan

....

....

....

....

....

....

....

....

....

....

....

....

....

....

....

The person with a safe center doesn't fear change.
You can choose change without fear before a challenge
only when you are strongly centered.

Day 17

Complete Solitude

When you have realized that life is suffering
punctuated by fleeting moments of happiness,
when you face unbearable emptiness, see it as a blessing.
Finally, you are on the path of your spiritual journey.

Day 17

Tomorrow's Plan

....

....

....

....

....

....

....

....

....

....

....

....

....

....

The loneliness of those who confront their lives
magnificently is beautiful. People who have felt
loneliness thoroughly, who have been alone completely,
can feel what wholeness is. Only those who have felt
wholeness in complete solitude can
find truth in everything.

Day 18

Becoming a Diamond

Between "I'll do it" and "I'll give it a try,"
there exists a difference so subtle as to be
barely distinguishable, yet so fundamental
as to determine the success or failure of an endeavor.

Day 18

Tomorrow's Plan

....

....

....

....

....

....

....

....

....

....

....

....

....

....

A diamond is just a lump of coal until it is turned
into a diamond through constant pressure.
Rather than becoming discouraged or destroyed
by the challenges you face, let them shape you
into a stronger, more refined human being.

Day 19

The Legacy

The people we meet in any context,
with whom we interact, work, and play,
are all partners for our growth. Just like us,
they are growing through their life's journey.

Day 19

Tomorrow's Plan

....
....
....
....
....
....
....
....
....
....
....
....
....
....
....
....
....

The most valuable legacy that we can pass on
to future generations is the recovery of our humanity,
so that they can experience a deeper
and more meaningful existence.

Day 20

One More Step

When you think you've reached the end
of the road, take one more step.
That one step will create a new road before you.

Day 20

Tomorrow's Plan

It's not enough to see light only for an instant.
That's only the beginning of enlightenment.
The soul needs training to grow.

Day 21

And Healing Begins

Let your passion be reflected in the spark in your eyes
and the lightness in your step, propelling you
beyond any obstacle, until you breathe
your final exhalation with a smile on your face.

Day 21

Tomorrow's Plan

....

....

....

....

....

....

....

....

....

....

....

....

....

....

As you progress on the soul's journey, you will encounter
the source of love and oneness that exists beyond
separation. You will come to know that this source exists
inside all others as well, for their discovery. Compassion
for yourself, for others, and for the Earth all flow out of
such awareness. And healing begins.

A New Journey Begins

Congratulations! Having come this far along in your 21-day training, you have already done a great deal to change the shape of your life. Even if you have not followed your plan perfectly, you have made great strides toward creating your ideal life. If you have learned anything about yourself through this process, then it has indeed been meaningful for you.

Regardless of your 21-day training goal and how well you achieved it, you have made a remarkable statement about yourself. Through it, you are saying to the world, "I believe in myself, and I know I can meet my potential."

Now is the time to consider what your 21-day training means to you. Hopefully, it will not just be filed away in the back of your mind as a nice educational experience. Rather, it should become a stepping-stone to greater and even more satisfying forms of your self-development.

Try to apply the same attitude to everyday life that you applied to your growth during this 21-day period. Any 21-day training is meant to be a self-contained, achievable approach to life management. But it is actually just a seed that can grow into a giant, branching tree of growth and endless possibility.

Focus on who you want to be and where you want to go with your life. Ask yourself the essential questions of life with as much honesty and sincerity as you can muster.

Ask, "Who am I?" and "What do I really want?" I challenge you to keep asking these questions until you no longer receive literal or conceptual answers.

If we approach these questions with deep effort and sincerity, they can penetrate straight through the masks of job, personality, ethnicity, gender, or any other ego reference.

Of course, it may take a great deal more self-reflection before you arrive at truly satisfactory answers, but the point is to begin living as though the answers to these questions are within reach. Apply your new understanding and awareness of yourself to your daily life. Move closer and closer, step by step, to the person you most want to become.

Su-haeng

We have come to this life for su-haeng*.
This world is the training ground of enlightenment.

Patience, forgiveness, and love
Are shortcuts to enlightenment and the growth of
consciousness.

To have given me these circumstances,
This is God's grace and love.

The body, relationships, and personality
And all the circumstances and time given to me,
These are the assignment and love given by my beloved.

A tree does not hold blame for being born on harsh land.
Whatever its kind, its environment, or how it becomes used,
With patience, forgiveness, and harmony,
it fulfills its mission.

What makes the mountain sacred and beautiful
Is that it does not judge any tree.
It accepts the rain as rain.
It accepts the wind as wind.
It accepts thunder as thunder.
When it snows, it accepts the snowfall.
It embraces all animals, and even people,
And it shows us patience, forgiveness, and love.

* Su-haeng means constant practical discipline of mind, body, and spirit.

Notes

....
....
....
....
....
....
....
....
....
....
....
....
....
....
....
....

Notes

Notes

Notes

Notes